BASED ON THE TRUE STORY OF THE FOUNDING OF THE ROMAN REPUBLIC

HORATIUS AT THE BRIDGE

RETOLD AND ILLUSTRATED BY MIKE BOLAN

Horatius

Captain of the bridge into Rome

Titus Herminius

Roman soldier. One of the "Dauntless Three"

Spurious Lartius

Roman soldier. Another of the "Dauntless Three"

Tiberinus

Moody river god

Astur the Huge

Etruscan soldier

Tarquin the Proud

King of Rome

Lars Porsena

Etruscan king

LinguaText Children's Classics #2

LinguaText, LLC
103 Walker Way
Newark, Delaware 19711

www.LinguaTextBooks.com
(302) 453-8695

ISBN: 978-0-942566-63-5

Manufactured in the United States of America

What if YOU were a KING?

When you're a king, you get to tell everyone what to do... plus you get a lot of free stuff! Just don't let it go to your head.

A long time ago, the land of Ancient Rome was ruled by a fellow called **King Tarquin**. As you might guess from the picture behind me, he was *not* a nice guy, and nobody likes a bully.

This was known as the **Age of Kings**...

I joined King Tarquin's army to keep my people safe in dangerous times, but I didn't like that Tarquin was a bully. I have to admit, I was happy on that day when the townsfolk of Rome became so fed up with Tarquin that they threw him out of the city—along with his rotten son!

My job is to guard this bridge into the city.

My name is Horatius... and this is my story!

So long!
HE's OUTTA HERE!
Daddy! My shoe!
I'll be back!
Let's go, son...
Buh-bye!
And stay out!
Take your nasty son with you!

After King Tarquin got kicked out of Rome, he whined, "I don't care if they *did* kick me out! I still want to be king!" So he went to the nearby kingdom of **Clusium** to visit his old friend **King Lars Porsena**.

In his kingly voice, King Lars Porsena said, "Don't worry, Tarquin, I'll help you. We can't have people getting rid of their kings, now, can we?"

King Lars Porsena gathered eighty thousand soldiers and countrymen — who were called **Etruscans**—to attack Rome so Tarquin could be king again. But they would have to cross the **Tiber River** to get to Rome, and it was storm season.

"Let's head for the bridge, everyone!" ordered King Lars Porsena. "Pay no attention to the Angry River God!"

It was said that the Tiber River was inhabited by a spirit called **Tiberinus**... and he was angry. That explained why the river was running high and fast.

I was guarding my bridge like usual, when out of a cloud of dust appeared a nervous scout on horseback. "To arms! To arms!" he cried.

He saw the town elders at the city gate and called to them, "Sir Consul: Lars Porsena is coming with his army!" The town elders looked to the east and saw the rising smoke of the approaching army in the distance, carrying the flag of Clusium.

"It was just a matter of time," said one of the council members. "The Etruscans and their giant warrior **Astur** have already conquered the hill at **Janiculum**."

"Horatius, your **Sublician Bridge** is the last bridge into Rome!" said the scout. "All the others have been taken down!" Addressing the council, the scout said "Well, Sir Lawrence, any ideas?!"

Lawrence the consul said "We have to save the city! Horatius, we should cut down this bridge, it's the last entrance into Rome!"

He was the first to grab an axe, and soldiers and townsfolk soon followed his lead. The brave citizens of Rome began chopping at the wooden bridge.

I heard a child say, "You'll never get the bridge down in time. The Etruscans are almost here. And there's a lot of 'em! Who can save us now?"

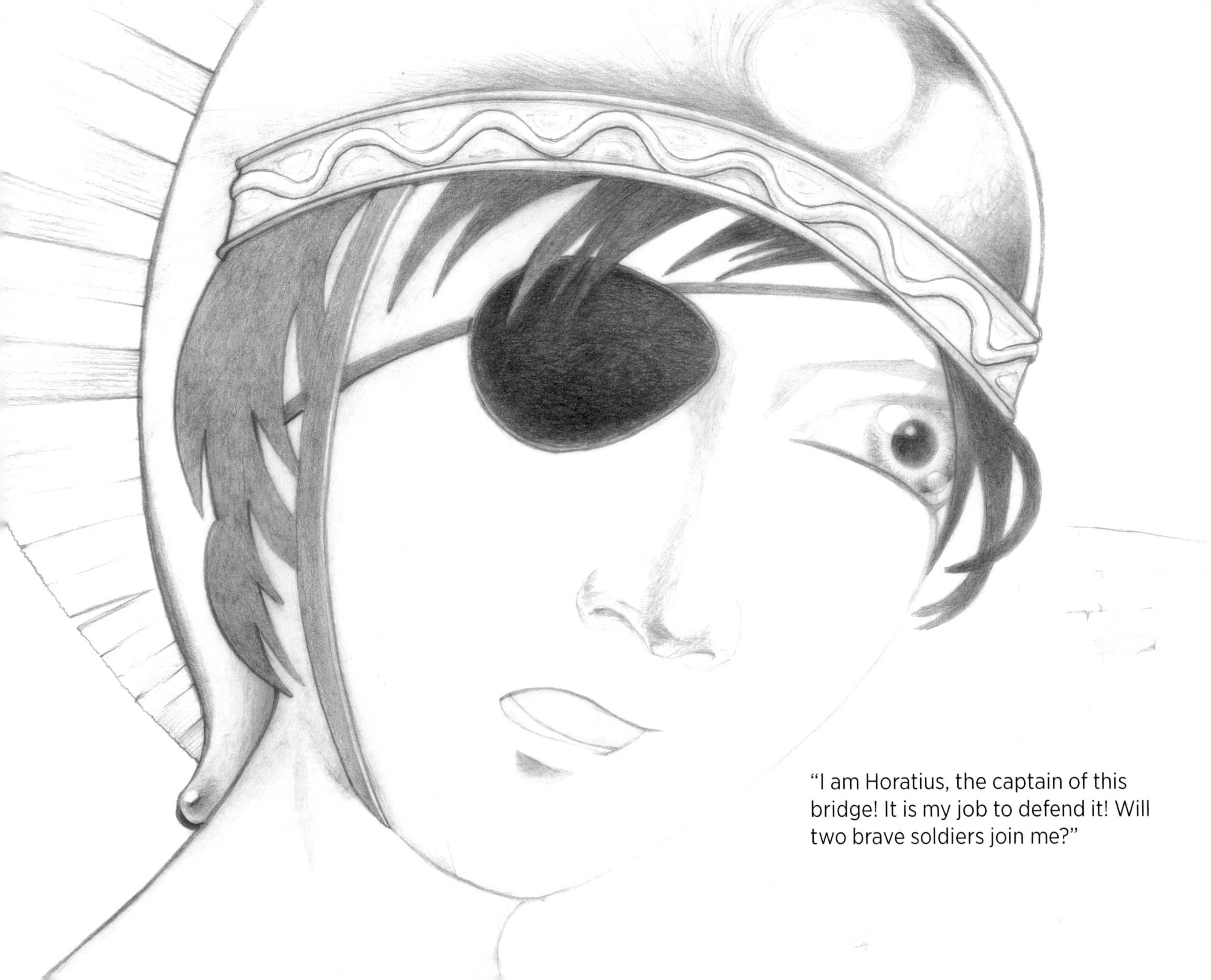

"I am Horatius, the captain of this bridge! It is my job to defend it! Will two brave soldiers join me?"

Unsure at first, two soldiers stepped forward. My old friend **Spurious Lartius** said, “I’ll fight with you, Horatius!”

The other soldier, **Titus Herminius**—inspired by the confidence of the others—said, “We’ll defend the bridge together. You can count on me!”

We crossed the bridge as our friends and families began to chop it down. The waves below seemed to be glaring up at us as they grew larger and fiercer. We were Rome's last defense!

They called us **the Dauntless Three**.

"What have we here?" sneered King Lars Porsena from his ivory chariot at the other side. "Those three puny soldiers think they can hold the bridge against MY mighty army!"

But the bridge wasn't wide enough for his entire army at once. Lars Porsena pointed at the Dauntless Three, snapped his fingers, and bellowed, "Take care of them!"

Immediately, three scowling Etruscan fighters brandished their swords and charged towards us. **Picus** growled at Lartius, who knocked him to the ground before tossing **Aunus** into the Tiber.

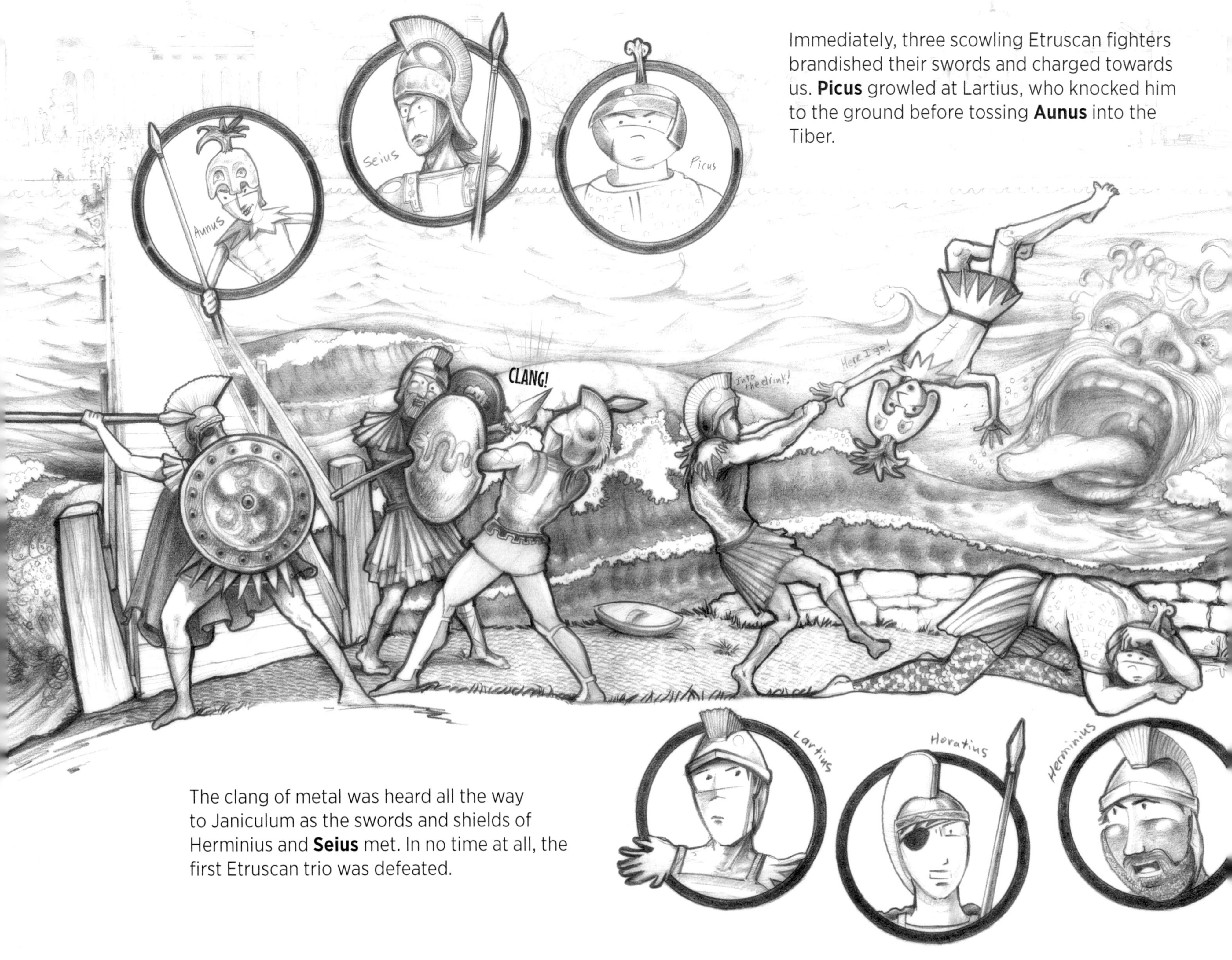

The clang of metal was heard all the way to Janiculum as the swords and shields of Herminius and **Seius** met. In no time at all, the first Etruscan trio was defeated.

“WHAT’S THIS?”

yelped King Lars Porsena as he looked at his devastated men. Then he turned to us and called,

“I see we have some warriors here! Send in the next three!”

From the other side of the Tiber River I heard a mighty **CHOP!** and one of the legs of the bridge fell into the water.

At Lars Porsena’s command, three more soldiers approached the bridge. They were even bigger than the previous three.

Even so, using their great strength and skill, Lartius and Herminius were able to outfight the next three. The crowd of Etruscans began to look worried. Lars Porsena yelled:

"WELL, IN THAT CASE..."

"...Where's Astur?"

...over here...

"Here I am," came a deep, thundering voice. It was **Astur**, the famous and gigantic hero of the Etruscans.

"I'll take care of these *Dauntless Three*!" he growled.

Drawing his sword, the enormous Astur approached the bridge. I gulped and stepped between Lartius and Herminius. "I've got this," I said.

Meanwhile, on the other side of the bridge...

SPLASH! Another leg of the bridge fell into the river.

Astur and I crossed swords and slammed our shields. I glared into his eyes and thought of my people in Rome. I could not let them live under the tyranny of an evil king ever again.

I blocked a brutal blow, but Astur's sword slid down and cut my leg! My leg stung and I fell backwards.

Spurius Lartius caught me.

Titus Herminius said,

"I'll stop him!"

"No!" I said to Titus Herminius. "Leave him to me!" I lunged into the air towards Astur, inspired by my desire to save my friends. My sword came down upon Astur's helmet with such a clang they could hear it in Janiculum. He would do no more fighting this day.

I yelled to the Etruscans, **"THAT is the welcome you will ALL get if you pass this bridge to Rome!"** Lars Porsena jumped from his chariot and shook his fists in the air.

With their champion defeated, the Etruscans began to seriously doubt victory.

They were confused; those in the back called to charge ahead, those in front called for retreat. Still, they had a huge army to send against me and Spurious Lartius and Titus Herminius. We were exhausted and a storm was approaching. At last I heard a sound that was music to my ears:

CRA-ACK! Finally, the bridge was **BEGINNING TO FALL!**

YES!
Well, I don't believe it!
The bridge is coming down!
Come back, Horatius!
We did it!
Uh-oh! Loose boards!

"Come back, Horatius! The bridge is collapsing!" the Romans called from the shore.

"Get back, Lartius! Get back, Herminius!" I commanded to my friends on the bridge. I knew that the Etruscans would still run across if I retreated now. I held the entire army back as my bridge started to fall into the raging river.

The storm was upon us!

It was as though the River God Tiberinus roared with anger when the thunder and lightning struck. When the bridge collapsed, I had no choice but to hold my breath and... jump!

I hit the water in full armor with a tremendous splash, and disappeared into the current.
Raising my shield above the waves, I gasped for air and began to swim back to Rome.
The disbelieving Etruscans hurled javelins at me as I swam. Luckily I still wore my helmet.
My leg was stinging where Astur had cut me, but I found the strength to keep swimming.

Spurius Lartius and Titus Herminius pulled me out of the charitable hands of Tiberinus as I reached the shore. The excited Romans danced and cheered and lit bonfires in celebration. Even the Etruscans on the other side cheered for my unlikely survival.

Rome was safe. King Lars Porsena sneered,

"It looks like Tiberinus is on their side today!"

"It must be an omen!" cried one of the Etruscans. They believed the gods were not on their side—and the river was favoring Rome today. The Sublician Bridge had fallen and the Etruscans didn't dare swim in the angry Tiber, so they went back to their homes in the Clusium countryside.

Neither Tarquin nor any king would rule over the Romans again, and the **Age of Kings** came to a close. The **Roman Republic** had begun! The people of the land would **elect** leaders to represent them.

My fellow citizens made a statue of me and put it right in the center of town.

They gave me as much land as a stout ox could plow in a day and enough food to last until my crops came in.

I married a sweet young lady and started a family.

Things were looking up for me, but with my injured leg from the bout with the gigantic Astur (not to mention that time I got poked in the eye...), I figured the gods were giving me hints to retire.

Nowadays, I simply work the fields with my trusty ox, although I'm always ready to protect the city. We are all grateful to have a say in how the city is run, here in the **Ancient Roman Republic**. I hope we can keep it this way. Lartius is even thinking of running for consul!

About the Story of *Horatius at the Bridge*

Thousands of years ago in what is now Italy, there was a real soldier named Horatius who defended the last bridge into Rome from invaders. It was the end of the Age of Kings, and Horatius helped usher in the Roman Republic, giving citizens power over their own society. In ancient times, people would sing songs and write poems about heroic and memorable events like this. The Roman historian Livy wrote a few paragraphs about it, but there was no epic poetic remembrance for the valiant one-eyed Horatius...

That is, until about two hundred years ago, when a man from England named Macauley read Livy's ancient account of Horatius and the events that led up to the start of the Roman Republic. Mr. Macauley decided to write a poem himself—in a style that *sounded* like it was written by Ancient Romans.

The book you hold in your hands was inspired by Livy's *History of Rome* and Macauley's 1842 *Lays of Ancient Rome*—a collection of narrative poems—one of which was called *Horatius at the Bridge*.

www.ingramcontent.com/pod-product-compliance
Ingram Content Group UK Ltd.
Pitfield, Milton Keynes, MK11 3LW, UK
UKRC031203030826
14089UKWH00035B/258

9780942566635